**Collins**

The Exam

by

Andy Hamilton

Resource Material by
Suzy Graham-Adriani
and
Anthony Banks

William Collins' dream of knowledge for all began with the publication of his first book in 1819. A self-educated mill worker, he not only enriched millions of lives, but also founded a flourishing publishing house. Today, staying true to this spirit, Collins books are packed with inspiration, innovation and a practical expertise. They place you at the centre of a world of possibility and give you exactly what you need to explore it.

Collins. Do more.

Published by Collins
An imprint of HarperCollins*Publishers*
77–85 Fulham Palace Road
Hammersmith
London
W6 8JB

Commissioned by Charlie Evans
Design by JPD
Cover design by Charlotte Wilkinson
Production by Katie Butler
Printed and bound by Imago in Singapore

Acknowledgements

Text credits: p84 "Exam Stress – and how to beat it" is taken from the Childline website: www.childline.org.uk

Photo credits: p70 © Simon Annand; p86 two posters for the play from NT Connections productions – Waterford Youth Drama and Looe Community School.

Browse the complete Collins catalogue at www.collinseducation.com

© HarperCollins*Publishers* Limited 2005

10 9 8 7 6 5

ISBN-13 978-0-00-720725-1
ISBN-10 0-00-720725-5

British Library Cataloguing in Publication Data

A Catalogue record for this publication is available from the British Library

Contents

Characters

Mr A	Andrew's dad
Mrs A	Andrew's mum
Mr B	Bea's dad
Mrs B	Bea's mum
Mrs C	Chas's mum
Andrew	sixteen years old
Bea	sixteen years old
Chas	sixteen years old
Miss Baxendale	Geography teacher invigilating the exam
Mr Biggs	PE teacher
Ex	voice of the exam
Dad	Chas's dad
Auntie Jean	Bea's auntie

The Exam

Scene One

A tight spotlight picks out a cluster of adults.

Mr and Mrs A (well dressed, moneyed, broadsheet-newspaper readers who probably spend a lot of time at the gym), Mr and Mrs B (clothing from BHS, like to stay in and watch detective series on television) and Mrs C (chaotic, single mother of four, bit heavy on the make-up, prone to leopard-skin print, hectic social life).

Physically, these five characters are in a tight group, but the eyelines of the two couples and single mum are all trained in slightly different directions. For a moment they form a still tableau, but then Mr A kicks them into a rat-tat-tat barrage of parental 'support'. (Mr A is dynamic, comically so; Mrs A is relentlessly positive; Mr and Mrs B are a two-headed, smothering pride-fest; and Mrs C is cursory and getting ready to go out.)

MR A	Always read the question.
MRS A	Always.
MR A	And read it carefully.
MRS A	Very carefully.
MR B	We know you'll do well.
MRS B	You always do well.
MRS C	Just try not to cock it up.
MR A	Keep an eye on the time.
MRS A	Don't spend too long…
MR A/MRS A	*(louder)* … on one question.

MR B	You're bound to do well.
MRS B	You're so good at exams.
MR B	Mr Pringle said so.
MRS B	At the parent's evening.
MR B	'She's brilliant at exams.'
MRS B	That's what he said.
MR B	'But then she's brilliant at everything.'
MRS B	His very words.
MRS C	I won't be in when you get back.
MRS B	'She's my star,' he said.
MRS C	You'll have to make tea for the others.
MR A	Take plenty of pens.
MRS C	I'm out line-dancing.
MRS A	Lots of pens.
MR A	You never know when a pen might let you down.
MRS A	True.
MR A	Pens are like that.
MR B	We'll be thinking of you.
MRS B	I've got éclairs for tea.
MR B	Celebration éclairs.
MRS C	Not sure what time I'll be back.
MR B	Good luck, dear.
MRS C	Don't let Ashley near the light sockets.
MRS B	Good luck, dear.

Mrs C	He might not be so lucky next time.
Mr A	I know exams are tough.
Mrs A	He does know, dear.
Mr A	Life is tough.
Mrs A	But exciting.
Mr A	Life's a jungle.
Mrs A	An exciting jungle.
Mr A	And if you're in the jungle…
Mrs A	… you want to be a cheetah, not a limping wildebeest.
Mrs C	Just do your best.
Mr B	We're so proud of you.
Mrs C	You can only do your best.
Mrs B	So very proud.
Mrs C	And if your best is still rubbish, well, there you go.
Mr A	Remember, don't panic.
Mrs A	Panic never helps.
Mr B	Don't worry.
Mrs B	We're not worried.
Mrs C	Don't mess about.
Mr A	Don't freeze.
Mrs	Don't rush.
Mr B	Don't worry.
Mrs B	Don't hurry.
All	And don't get nervous!

Snap blackout.

Slowly the lights come up on three schoolchildren sitting side by side on three chairs.

Andrew *is sixteen, bookish, his school uniform is immaculate and he is relentlessly studying his notes as he crams in some last-minute revision. He is a martyr to teenage spots. Next to him is* **Bea**, *also sixteen, a little self-conscious but very bright. She is looking out into space, trying to stay calm, but she throws a telltale glance at her watch. Next to her is* **Chas**, *also sixteen. His school uniform is very untidy and his left arm is in a sling. He looks around, bored. This is a guy with a short attention span. He looks at* **Bea**, *trying to make eye contact, but she keeps looking out straight. He makes a quiet popping sound with his lips. Neither of the other two respond. He leans back a bit and stares at the ceiling for a while, then sits up again.*

CHAS   *(suddenly breaking into a motor-racing commentator impersonation)* And the tension here is unbelievable. You could, quite literally, cut it with a knife.

He gets no reaction from the other two, apart from **Bea** *shifting her bodyweight and angling herself away from him slightly. Another awkward silence develops.* **Chas** *hunts for an ice-breaking topic.*

   So... how would you defeat global terrorism, then?

Slowly **Bea** *turns and looks at him with withering disdain.*

   Just trying to make conversation.

BEA   Well don't.

Bea angles herself away from him again. Another awkward silence. **Chas** *slaps his thighs to a rhythm, puffs his cheeks, stares at the ceiling and generally tries various displacement activities before chancing his next gambit.*

CHAS   Adults are such prossocks, aren't they?

10

Again, no flicker of a response. The statement just hangs in the air.

> Yup… Total prossocks.

BEA   'Prossocks'?

CHAS   Yeah.

BEA   What sort of a word is 'prossock'?

CHAS   It's one of my words.

BEA   You have your own words?

CHAS   Yeah, how cool is that?

Bea shakes her head and quietly mutters something as she turns her back on Chas. For the first time, Andrew looks up from his notes.

ANDREW   *(sounding unnaturally middle-aged)* Jesus wept, where has that bloody woman got to? It's a disgrace.

BEA   I know.

ANDREW   I mean, where's she gone to find this key – Vladivostok? She's taken *(checks watch)* fourteen and a half minutes. That woman's a nightmare.

CHAS   She's a prossock.

ANDREW   What's a prossock?

CHAS   A prat, a tosser and a pillock rolled into one. Prossock. I have my own slang, see, because normal slang dates really quick, doesn't it?

BEA   *(trying to be aloof)* Is that right?

CHAS   Oh yeah, like, the other day Terry Doyle came out with 'wicked' and everyone just stared at him like he was a complete twonklet. Have you got a boyfriend?

BEA	(with lawyer-like precision) No, I do not have a boyfriend. I do not want or need a boyfriend, but if I do decide to have a boyfriend he won't be someone who says things like 'twonklet.'
CHAS	It's your loss, baby.

Bea gets up and walks away, muttering something uncomplimentary.

ANDREW	Where has the woman go to? We should have started these exams *(checks watch)* fifteen and a half minutes ago.
CHAS	What are you taking?
ANDREW	Resitting History GCSE, I, um… well, there was a bit of a hiccup.
CHAS	*(sensing there's a story behind this)* Oh… I see. I'm doing Maths GCSE. Should have been last Thursday, but I was down the hospital having my collarbone seen to. *(indicates his arm in a sling)* Maths is the only one I stand a chance of getting, really. I'm not bad with numbers. But anything that involves writing words, well I've got this problem, y'see?
ANDREW	Dyslexic?
CHAS	No, just thick. What exam are you taking, Two-Brains.
BEA	*(icily)* Please don't call me that.
CHAS	Don't get in a strop, they only call you Two-Brains on account of you being a genius. It's a compliment. And anyway, there are worse nicknames, aren't there, Zitboy?

Andrew stiffens at the use of his nickname.

That's what they call you, isn't it, Zitboy? I heard Toby Pearce calling you that in the playground.

	Mind you, he can talk, his face looks like it's been pebble-dashed. What's your real name?
ANDREW	Andrew.
CHAS	Classy.
ANDREW	*(looks at watch)* Where has she got to?
CHAS	And-rew. Not Andy. And-rew.
BEA	Oh, she'll be ages yet. You know how she went to pieces when she discovered the room was locked. She'll have gone into one of her flaps. I've seen her do it hundreds of times. She's my form mistress. We call her BSE.
ANDREW	BSE?
BEA	'Cos she's a dizzy cow.
ANDREW	Oh, right.
CHAS	*(apropos of nothing in particular)* Mr Biggsy's my form teacher.
BEA	She's sleeping with him.
CHAS	I know. Gary Spackman took a Polaroid of the pair of them playing tongue-hockey behind the CCF hut… *(worried)* Funny bloke, Gary.
ANDREW	But Mr Biggs is married, isn't he?
BEA	Oh yes.
ANDREW	Well then, they shouldn't be having a relationship. I mean, that's totally unprofessional.
CHAS	No, it's only unprofessional if it affects the quality of their work. *(to **Andrew**)* Who's your form teacher?
ANDREW	We haven't got one at the moment. It was Henderson. Till he had that breakdown.

CHAS	*(remembering)* Oh… yeah… he looked quite funny naked, didn't he? Had sort of sticky-out nipples.
ANDREW	Look at the time. This is scandalous. *(he starts to pace)*
CHAS	The man's right.

*There is another pause as they think their own thoughts, till **Chas** punctures it.*

*(to **Bea**)* How old were you… the day you first realised that adults were useless?

She doesn't answer.

I worked out you couldn't rely on them when I was six. My dad bet his mate that tortoises could swim and, well, that's how I lost my pet tortoise.

ANDREW	*(checks watch)* Seventeen minutes! I mean, this is our future she's jeopardising. My mental preparation for this exam is completely shot now, I was pacing myself… Mental preparation is the key.

*Hard cut to a tight spotlight where **Mr A** (Andrew's dad) is giving a pep talk.*

MR A	Mental preparation is the key, son. That's a fact. It's what gives you the edge. It's probably where you went wrong last time when you… *(he stops himself.)* Come here.

Andrew *crosses and enters the tight spot.* **Mr A** *wraps his arms around* **Andrew** *and hugs him hard with possessive affection.*

Listen, tiger, this isn't just one more exam, this… this is when you find out about yourself.

Mrs A *joins them to form a group hug.*

14

	It's about character. About bouncing back from disaster and proving something to yourself. About walking back into the sunlight, having stared down into the abyss.
MRS A	Think of it as an adventure.
MR A	Now, let's see you bounce, eh, tiger?

*Immediate lights-up as **Andrew** crosses to rejoin **Bea** and **Chas**.*

ANDREW	I mean, is it really so much to ask? That candidates for exams should be able to access the exam room? Jesus! *(winces slightly)* Um… I'll be back in a minute. *(exits)*
BEA	I wish he wouldn't say 'Jesus' all the time.
CHAS	Are you a Christian?
BEA	No, I just believe all religious faiths should be respected.
CHAS	What, even Jehovah's Witnesses?
BEA	Yes.
CHAS	Oh, right. Are you sure you don't want a boyfriend?
BEA	I told you.
CHAS	Only I've always quite rated you.
BEA	I am so not interested in this conversation.
CHAS	Every time you go up on stage to get one of your prizes I say to my mates, 'I quite rate her'.
BEA	I feel honoured.
CHAS	And rightly so. Mind you. I preferred you before you got skinny.
BEA	I haven't got 'skinny'.

CHAS	You have. I mean, granted, you're not as skinny as some of the other girls in your form have got... not yet anyway.
BEA	I'm not obsessing about my diet, if that's what you're saying.
CHAS	I'm pleased to hear it.
BEA	I'm merely aiming to achieve my ideal bodyweight.
CHAS	Fair enough, do you want some Kit-Kat? *(produces Kit-Kat)*
BEA	No, thank you.

*Hard lighting change to **Mr** and **Mrs B** (her parents).*

MRS B	Some cake, then?
BEA	*(crossing to join them)* I don't want cake, Mum.
MRS B	Well you've got to eat something.
BEA	I eat plenty.
MR B	We've got éclairs. You deserve an éclair. All that revision you've been doing.
MRS B	And chocolate's good for the brain. It was on *Richard and Judy*.
BEA	*(with a hint of snobbery)* Richard and Judy?
MRS B	Yes.
BEA	I'm going up to my room. *(Exits.)*
MR B	*(calling after her)* I'll bring you up a cocoa.

Mr and Mrs B exchange a look. They wish they could bridge the distance between themselves and their daughter.

*The light picks out **Bea** and **Chas**, as before.*

CHAS	*(eating)* How many calories in a Kit-Kat, then?
BEA	About 320.
CHAS	But who's counting, eh, Two-Brains?

*Bea looks at him as he pops the last bit of Kit-Kat into his mouth. She is just not sure what to make of him. **Andrew** re-enters, looking a little pale.*

	You okay?
ANDREW	Nervous tummy.

*Rather gingerly, **Andrew** picks up his revision notes and tries to concentrate on them.*

CHAS	I wouldn't bother with any last-minute swotting if I was you…
ANDREW	Really.
CHAS	Yeah, in my experience, if you don't know it by now, you never will.
BEA	Oh, so you're an expert on passing exams then, are you?
CHAS	I never said I'd passed any. I just said that in my experience, if you didn't know it by now, you never will. And my results bear that out.

***Andrew** suddenly closes his revision notes.*

ANDREW	You're probably right… making me feel nauseous… *(looks around, hunting for a topic)* How did you break your collarbone?
CHAS	Very painfully. Do you know Spike Morton?
ANDREW	Morton? Is he the one with the tattoo saying 'Babe Magnet'?
CHAS	That's right, on his left buttock.

*There is a snort of disdain from **Bea**.*

Spike lives near me, so we go home together after school. Anyway, we've got this game we like to play where I shout abuse at passers-by and then he tells them that I suffer from Tourette's Syndrome. It's great fun. You can get away with murder. My favourite was when I saw this bunch of nuns and I started yelling that they were 'giant nympho killer penguins'.

***Andrew** laughs, a kind of kinship is springing up between them. **Bea**, meanwhile, is working very hard at pretending not to listen.*

So, last Wednesday this chubby bloke walked past and I shouted, 'You big fat git' and, well, he didn't take it very well, got a bit upset. But then Spike weighs in and goes, 'Calm down, mate, no offence, he didn't mean it, he's got Tourette's.' And so this fat bloke goes, 'Oh, right, okay, no problem,' and starts to back off, and Spike goes, 'He didn't mean to call you a big fat git, mister, he meant to call you an ugly fat git.' Then we both legged it as fast as we could up the High Street.

ANDREW	So, what happened then?
CHAS	Well… you know fat people aren't supposed to be very good at running?
ANDREW	He caught up with you.
CHAS	Well, he would have done, if we hadn't had the brains to climb up this scaffolding, 'cos both me and Spike are so hot at climbing, so we ended up two storeys high with the Michelin man down below, puffing and wheezing, shaking his fist and stuff. So, we taunted him a bit more about… y'know… about his… not having achieved his ideal bodyweight. *(**Bea** stiffens)* Then, and with hindsight this was a mistake, we started singing. *(sings)* 'Who ate all the pies? Who ate all the

pies? You fat bastard, you fat bastard, you ate all the pies.'

ANDREW	Then what?
CHAS	Well… you know fat people aren't supposed to be any good at climbing?
ANDREW	Oh no.
CHAS	Like a sodding monkey he was. Coming straight for us. Well, Spike was panicking, but I spotted this way down, namely on one of those sort of orange waste chutes that hang down off scaffolding into skips…
ANDREW	*(realising)* You prat.
CHAS	I've seen people doing it on the telly. That girl, Caroline Thingy, she jumped down one in an episode of *Jonathan Creek,* and all that happened to her was she got a bit dusty. I just thought it'd be like, I dunno, like a helter-skelter at the fairground, only maybe a bit quicker. Anyway, it was, um, well it was quite a lot quicker, actually. The bloke in Casualty said I'm lucky I didn't kill myself. Then he said something I didn't quite catch but it ended with the words 'stupid cretin'.
ANDREW	Jesus, what did your parents say?
CHAS	My mum got a bit emotional…

Snap lighting transition to the parental zone where **Mrs C** *(Chas's mum) is getting ready to go out.* **Chas** *crosses to join her as she talks. Every now and then she shouts over her shoulder to invisible offspring.*

MRS C	Well, this is very inconvenient. How are you going to help me out with one arm? *(Shouts off)* Ashley, get your fingers away from that socket! *(to* **Chas***)* What you've done is stupid, reckless and unhelpful. *(shouts)* Sacha! Come down here, I'm sending you up the chip shop! *(to* **Chas***)* What the hell were you… *(shouts)* Ashley, I

won't tell you again. *(to **Chas**)* What the hell were you doing? You could have killed yourself. What would I have done then? *(shouts)* Ashley, if you don't get your fingers away from that socket I'll chop them off, so help me God! *(to **Chas**)* Oh, so now he starts crying, brilliant. *(shouts)* Sacha! I'm leaving the money on the table! *(to **Chas**)* All right, you take it easy, you silly sod. *(she brushes her hand against his cheek.)* You are such a silly sod... Okay, gotta dash. Can you help Gary with his homework? It's algebra or something.

CHAS   He's going purple, Mum.

MRS C   Ignore him, that's just an attention thing. I might be late, so don't put the bolt on. Be good, you silly sod, try not to fling yourself down the stairs, don't wait up. *(she kisses him on the cheek and then is gone)*

---

*Lighting transition as **Chas** crosses stage to rejoin **Bea** and **Andrew**.*

CHAS   So... that was Mum's reaction. *(a thought dawns)* At least... that's how I remember her reaction... it was something like that.

ANDREW   And what did your dad say?

CHAS   Not a lot, he's dead.

ANDREW   Oh... I'm sorry.

CHAS   Yeah, well... there you go. Four years ago now.

BEA   What happened?

CHAS   Well, he was always a bit of a vague person, y'know, daydreamer, forgetful and um... well one day he forgot to look and got hit by a bus.

BEA   Oh...

CHAS   Yeah.

ANDREW   Where did the bus hit him?

20

Chas looks at Andrew in bewilderment.

CHAS   … All over…

ANDREW   No, sorry, I didn't mean where on his body, I
                  meant where? What street?

CHAS   Oh right, sorry, Cambridge Circus. It's a well-
                  known black spot, only the victims are usually
                  just tourists.

ANDREW   Do you miss him?

CHAS   'Course, but I still see him a fair bit, y'know.

BEA   You still see him?

CHAS   Yeah, his ghost comes to visit me.

BEA   Your dad's ghost?

CHAS   Yeah.

BEA   This is a wind-up, right?

CHAS   No.

BEA   *(certain it's a wind-up)* So, when your dad's ghost
                  appears to you, what does he look like?

CHAS   Like Dad.

BEA   I mean, what does he wear?

CHAS   Well, white stuff obviously, he's a ghost.

BEA   *(laughs, mocking)* Oh right, white stuff, yeah,
                  'course.

CHAS   You don't believe me, do you, Two-Brains?

BEA   I'm a rational person, I don't believe in ghosts.

ANDREW   People do see things, though, don't they? My
                  mum saw the shape of a woman at a B and B in
                  Margate.

BEA	People convince themselves they see things. It's just projections from their subconscious mind. He doesn't have a ghost, he's having you on. He's smirking.

*From offstage we hear an approaching apologetic voice. It is **Miss Baxendale**. She is as nervous as a small bird and her self-confidence is brittle. She is carrying a Polaroid camera.*

MISS BAXENDALE	Sorry, sorry everybody, sorry to take so long, but everything's under control, sorry.
ANDREW	Have you got the key?
MISS BAXENDALE	Well, it seems our beloved caretaker has wandered off with the keys. He's always doing that, gives him a sense of power, but nil desperandum, the trusty Mr Biggs is locating the spare. So all shall be well. Sorry about this, you'll get your full allotted time, of course, but I'm sorry about the… Sorry *(she starts to look out for **Mr Biggs**. She clears her throat with a nervous cough)*
CHAS	Why are you holding a Polaroid, miss?
MISS BAXENDALE	Eh? Oh, um, I confiscated this off, oh whatsisname, Gary Spackman. He's always bringing this in, he's been warned. Anyway, I gave him a week's worth of detentions.
CHAS	I'm not sure that was a good idea, miss.
MISS BAXENDALE	*(still looking out for **Mr Biggs**)* What?
CHAS	Well, I just don't think Gary Spackman is someone you want to get the wrong side of.
MISS BAXENDALE	What are you talking about, you strange boy?
ANDREW	*(looks as if he's really suffering)* Where's Mr Biggs gone to get this spare key?
MISS BAXENDALE	Don't fret, he's… Are you okay, Andrew, are you in pain?

ANDREW	I'm okay.
MISS BAXENDALE	Is it the ulcer?
ANDREW	*(irritated by her indiscretion)* I'm okay.
MISS BAXENDALE	Well say if you're not.
ANDREW	I will.
MISS BAXENDALE	Because you don't have to sit this, y'know, given what you...
ANDREW	*(cuts her off)* I'm okay! Okay?
MISS BAXENDALE	Okay.

There is an awkward pause as they wait for **Mr Biggs**.

> Mr Biggs will be here is a mo... He's a good man in a crisis...

The kids just watch her. She becomes self-conscious. She does some more involuntary nervous throat clearing.

> *(referring to the camera)* Just going to dump this in the staff room.

She exits busily. **Bea** *and* **Chas** *look at* **Andrew**.

CHAS	You've got an ulcer?
ANDREW	Yes.
BEA	A stomach ulcer?
ANDREW	Yes.
CHAS	*(with disbelief)* You're sixteen years old and you've got an ulcer?
ANDREW	Yes.
CHAS	You have to be middle-aged at least to get an ulcer. What, have you got a mortgage as well? And a wide selection of cardigans?

ANDREW	I can't help it. Ulcers run in the family. It's to do with tension. When I'm tense, I make acid.
CHAS	Then don't get tense. Learn to hang loose. *(Starts jive-talking and moonwalking.)* Stay cool, babe, find your groove.
BEA	Ignore him, he's a twat.
ANDREW	*(to Bea)* I try not to get tense. I try so hard. Hardly slept for months.
BEA	Have you learnt to unwind? What do you do for fun?
ANDREW	*(thinks hard)* Erm… nothing really. *(remembers)* Oh, I read biking magazines. I love Harley Davidsons, see. They're fantastic things. I know every inch of a Harley Davidson. I'm going to own one some day. And the leathers, with the eagle's-wings badge, and my name picked out in studs. *(his face is bright with enthusiasm, but suddenly all the confidence seems to drain out of him)* Well, that's if everything goes okay and I can afford it and I pass the driving test and stuff… Got to get through this first. *(he slumps with his head in his hands)* You heard what happened to me I suppose?
CHAS	No.
ANDREW	*(surprised)* Oh, funny, I just presumed everyone would have heard.
BEA	Why, what did happen to you?
ANDREW	*(very depressed)* I humiliated myself.
CHAS	*(trying to make him feel better)* Oh, we've all done that. *(looks to Bea for support)* Eh? Actually you probably haven't have you? *(throws it back to himself)* But I have. Made a pratt of myself dozens of times. It's not important. People forget.
BEA	*(to Andrew)* What happened?

ANDREW	I was supposed to sit this with the rest of my History set last Thursday, and I was all ready. I'd been up most of the night, memorising all my notes about Palmerston and Disraeli and the Tolpuddle sodding Martyrs... but the moment I turned over my exam paper... none of the words seemed to join up... and it wasn't just the words... nothing looked joined up... even the legs of the chairs didn't seem to be connected to the floor. Everything seemed... dislocated... and everyone's faces looked sort of jagged, with mouths like... like the mouths of broken bottles. Then everything started to spin and I woke up in the Nurse's Room.
CHAS	That is major-league scary.
ANDREW	What's really scary is I've no way of knowing if it'll happen again.
BEA	But, why are you resitting this today?
ANDREW	Well my dad persuaded the Head to ask if I could resit. He got them to say I'd reacted adversely to some hayfever medicine.
BEA	No, I meant why the hell are you resitting it today? You're obviously still in a state. Why put yourself through this? You could resit next term.
ANDREW	No... no, I have to face it now.
BEA	Says who?

*Hard lighting transition to **Mr A** on his feet, animated with **Mrs A** hovering nervously behind. As he talks, **Andrew** crosses to join him.*

MR A	You have to face this now. You can't run away. All right, you lost it, you panicked, you fell off the horse, but the answer is to jump straight back on the horse... It's the only way... otherwise you'll just spend your whole life... *(runs out of metaphor)*... scared of horses.

ANDREW	… I'm allergic to horses.
MR A	No, look, the horses are just a… Forget the horses, look it's about… it's about mental strength, son… because… look, let me tell you something… You're feeling the pressure with all these exams, that's normal, of course it is, and you blew a bit of a fuse, that can happen, and you're probably looking forward to the day when you can wave goodbye and not have to go through any more exams. Am I right?
ANDREW	Yes, absolutely right.
MR A	Yeah, well, get this… the exams never stop… life is an exam. I face an exam every day at work… I have to achieve a pass mark… maintain good grades, outperform my fellow examinees, or colleagues, I have an invigilator, my immediate boss, Hugh Steepleton, and an Examining Board… Head Office. And everyone is sitting this continuous exam… and it's that pressure that makes us stronger, helps us compete… and you have to compete because believe me, son, it is brutal out there… it's a piranha-filled river… and if you live in a piranha-filled river… you're better off being a piranha.

Both **Andrew** and **Mrs A** look bewildered, even a little scared, by **Mr A**'s bleak take on life.

MRS A	Who fancies a cup of tea?
ANDREW	Piranha don't compete, though, do they?
MR A	What?
ANDREW	Well, at least, a piranha doesn't compete with other piranha.
MR A	Look…
ANDREW	Piranha are successful because they hunt communally in shoals.

MR A	Yes, but they have to compete with, the crocodiles and the alligators and look, forget the piranha, okay? That was just... *(to **Mrs A**)* The boy is so literal... Look, tiger... *(he puts his hands affectionately, if a little firmly, on **Andrew**'s shoulders)* I'm not asking you to do this for me... You have to do it for yourself.
MRS A	*(tentatively)* He could resit it next term.
MR A	Yes, he could. *(to **Andrew**)* But you'd know you chickened out... you'd carry that sense of shame inside for ever... and it'll eat away at you... Believe me... shame is corrosive... Now you're at a crossroads here... there's a path marked 'weak' and a path marked 'strong'... Which are you going to choose?

*Snap lighting transition to **Bea** and **Chas**.*

BEA	Does your dad really talk like that?
ANDREW	Yeah. *(he crosses back to **Bea** and **Chas**)* He's a bit... um...
CHAS	*(trying to be helpful)* Full of crap?
ANDREW	But he's not, though, is he? He's right. I have to face up to things, I don't want everyone knowing I bottled out... I don't want to know that...
BEA	But...
ANDREW	And if I wimp out again I'll just spend my life wimping out and being even more of a failure.
BEA	Yes, but what if it happens ag–
ANDREW	Look, just leave me alone, okay! I can do this! *(he walks away with his fingers pressed to his temples)* It is simply a question of being focused.

Andrew has now put some distance between himself and the other two. There is a pause, an awkward pause. Chas slaps out a rhythm on his thigh, stares at the ceiling for a bit...

CHAS   Are you sure you don't want to go on a date with me?

BEA   I said no, didn't I?

CHAS   I know, I just couldn't believe it. *(looks off to one side)* Not now Dad.

BEA   ... What?

CHAS   Oh, my dad's ghost just appeared. Over there. You can't see him, of course. He often pops up when I'm talking to a girl. He likes to coach me on when to make a move and stuff.

BEA   That isn't funny. Just tacky.

CHAS   *(talking off again)* Look, Dad, later, okay? This is a bit of a bad moment. Yeah – *(thumbs up)* – cheers.

BEA   Do I look like a gullible idiot?

CHAS   No, but then looks can be deceiving, can't they?

*We hear some nervy twittering from offstage and **Miss Baxendale** enters with a rather taciturn **Mr Biggs**. **Mr Biggs** is wearing a tracksuit and has the unmistakeably sarcastic bent of a PE teacher.*

MISS BAXENDALE   Sorry, sorry kids, crisis over, our knight in shining armour is here with the key, tra-la. Sorry to muck you about. Mr Biggs had trouble locating the key to the cupboard with the spare keys in.

Mr Biggs is a long way downstage, miming trying the key in the door.

MR BIGGS   It's that joke of a caretaker, he should be fired.

MISS BAXENDALE   Yes, Michael... sorry.

28

MR BIGGS   *(having some difficulty with the key)* I shouldn't
                   have to waste time doing this, I'm supposed to be
                   overseeing 3B's trampolining. Damn and blast!

MISS BAXENDALE Is there a problem?

Miss Baxendale comes downstage next to Mr Biggs.

MR BIGGS   This key's a crap key, surprise surprise, like every
                   crap thing in this crappy place.

*Miss Baxendale and Mr Biggs are now physically very close together
downstage. She drops her voice to try to prevent Andrew, Bea and Chas
(behind) overhearing.*

MISS BAXENDALE Have you told her yet?

MR BIGGS   *(also under his breath)* Now's not the time, Emily.

Miss Baxendale turns to the kids and gives them a reassuring smile.

MISS BAXENDALE Sorry about this silly old key, kids. *(she turns back
                   to Mr Biggs and drops her voice again)* You said you
                   were going to tell her.

MR BIGGS   I said, not now.

MISS BAXENDALE Or maybe you don't want to tell her.

MR BIGGS   Please, Emily, don't crowd me.

MISS BAXENDALE You said you'd tell her.

MR BIGGS   *(snaps, raising his voice)* I said don't crowd me!

*They become aware that Bea, Andrew and Chas are listening in, but when
they turn to look, the kids feign casual disinterest, study their shoes.*

                   (thrown) I... I can't turn this key if you crowd
                   me.

MISS BAXENDALE Oh... sorry. *(She backs off a few paces.)*

MR BIGGS	In fact *(still trying the key)* I can't turn this key... because, joy of joys, it's the wrong key, isn't it.
MISS BAXENDALE	*(approaching)* Oh, you're kidding.
MR BIGGS	This is Room 6 and, voila, a key labelled 6, but is it the right one? Oh no, that would be too much to expect. Heaven forfend, we can't have that.
BEA	Perhaps it's a nine.
MR BIGGS	*(stopped in his tracks)* ... What?
BEA	Perhaps it isn't a six, perhaps it's a nine.
MISS BAXENDALE	*(examining the label on the key)* You know, I think she might be right, I think it's a nine.
MR BIGGS	*(even more scornful)* Well, I'm sorry, but that is totally pathetic. Are you telling me you can tell that that's a nine and not a six just from looking at it?
MISS BAXENDALE	Well I...
MR BIGGS	There should be a little line scored under or over the digit, shouldn't there? Because, funnily enough, nine and six resembling each other is not a recently observed phenomenon.
MISS BAXENDALE	*(a bit upset)* Well, never mind, it's an easy mistake to make.
MR BIGGS	*(now in sarcasm overdrive)* Yes, it is an easy mistake, especially when nobody bothers to denote whether it's a six or a nine, either with a little line of with the number spelt out in brackets alongside, which is what they would do in an establishment that wasn't run by complete amateurs!
MISS BAXENDALE	*(her eyes welling up with tears)* I'm not responsible for numbering the keys, Michael.
MR BIGGS	Yes, yes, I know.

MISS BAXENDALE *(starting to lose it)* It's really not my area, I'm just a Geography teacher.

MR BIGGS Yes, yes, all right.

MISS BAXENDALE Just a small cog in a very big wheel. *(She bursts into tears.)*

Wearily **Mr Biggs** *takes her in his arms.*

MR BIGGS All right, all right.

ANDREW *(under his breath)* Hell, I don't believe this.

MR BIGGS *(with* **Miss Baxendale** *still crying on his shoulder)* Come on, old girl… *(**Mr Biggs** is thoroughly embarrassed by this show of emotion and very aware of being watched)* Come on, fruitdrop… chin up, eh?

MISS BAXENDALE I'm sorry, Michael… I've, um, I've been feeling a bit fragile.

MR BIGGS All right, all right, let's get you to the staff room and give you a cup of tea while I sort out this key nonsense. *(as he leads he off, he casually calls over his shoulder)* Okay, you lot, I'll be back in a tick, in the meantime, just… relax.

Mr Biggs leads Miss Baxendale off. Andrew stands open-mouthed with disbelief.

ANDREW We could sue them for this, y'know. This is mental torture. We could take them to the European Court of Human Rights.

BEA Try not to get too worked up. At the end of the day, it is just an exam.

ANDREW *(feeling patronised)* Yeah, well, that's easy for you to say, isn't it, Two-Brains? You just have to fart and you get an A.

BEA That is so gross.

CHAS	Very vulgar.
BEA	Yes.
CHAS	True though.
BEA	What?
CHAS	Well, it is sort of revolting how easy you find exams. How do you manage that. What's your secret?
BEA	I don't have a secret.
CHAS	You don't feel pressure, right?
BEA	Of course I feel pressure, I'm not a robot.
CHAS	Well then, how do you do it?
BEA	Well, um, basically, I suppose I just approach the exam as if… well, as if it was a sort of… big game.

Andrew turns and stares at her, appalled.

ANDREW	A game?
BEA	Yes.
ANDREW	*(sits, demoralised)* She treats it as a game.
BEA	For instance, when I read the question on the exam paper, I imagine I hear them in a voice. And the voice is a smooth, slightly sinister voice, y'know, like a baddie in a James Bond movie.
CHAS	Oh what, like Goldfinger? *(as Sean Connery)* Do you exshpect me to talk? *(as Goldfinger)* No, Mr Bond, I expect you to die!
BEA	Well no, the voice I hear is more like Christopher Lee in *The Man With the Golden Gu*n, or whatsisname, the one in *Thunderball*, Blofeld. Anyway, this 'voice' is my adversary and my job in the exams is to come up with the right

	answers and generally outwit and confound him.
ANDREW	*(to himself)* A game. She treats it as a game. *(suddenly his face lengthens)* Oh, no.
CHAS	What is it?
ANDREW	I think I'm going to be sick.
BEA	You think you're going to?
ANDREW	Yeah, not sure... Could go either way... Oh, God.
BEA	Think of something nice.
ANDREW	*(distressed)* Oooh.
BEA	Think of Harley Davidsons.
CHAS	He might feel better if he throws up.
ANDREW	Oh, hang on... wait... I think it's going to pass... *(turns queasy again)* Maybe not... it's borderline... I hate this feeling.
CHAS	Think of school custard.

Andrew stiffens, very tense, on the brink.

	Think of the lumps.

Andrew bolts offstage.

BEA	That wasn't very kind.
CHAS	Yes, it was. Better he throws up now than over his exam. Examiners don't like marking papers with little bits of carrot stuck to them.
BEA	Oh p-lease. I do so not want to hear this.
CHAS	Why do you talk like that?
BEA	Like what?
CHAS	Like you're in an episode of *Friends*.

BEA	Well why do you talk like you're in an episode of *The Cocky Moron Show*?
CHAS	Very good... I hate *Friends*.
BEA	Well, I like it.
CHAS	What, 'cos it's full of skinny girls? I suppose you like *Ally McBeal* as well.
BEA	My taste in television programmes is none of your business, actually.
CHAS	Yeah, you do like it.
BEA	Ally McBeal is a complex, funny, modern female character.
CHAS	She's an X-ray with lips.
BEA	*(hunts for a put-down)* Oh... go plummet down a chute.

*She turns away from **Chas** to freeze him out. He sits down two chairs away from her.*

CHAS	You never told me how you'd solve global terrorism.

She pointedly doesn't respond.

Look, I'm sorry I wound you up, I'm a wind-up merchant. Can't help myself... I'm a bit wound up too... Maths is the only paper I stand a chance of doing well in... and it's be nice to do well... if only for the novelty value.

***Bea** gives him half a smile.*

Are you resitting like him, then? Or did you miss one or something?

BEA	*(a little self-conscious)* No, I'm... I'm sitting an A-Level.

CHAS	What, two years early?
BEA	Yeah, Mr Pringle said I need to stretch myself.
CHAS	Did he? What's the subject?
BEA	Sociology.

Chas clearly has no idea what Sociology is. (And who has?)

CHAS	Ah, right, yeah, Sociology… the study of… sociologs.

Bea laughs.

> Yeah, well, 'course I nearly chose Sociology, but in the end I opted for the intellectual challenge of Woodwork.

The ice is now broken between them.

> Why aren't you sitting it with the Sixth Formers?

BEA	None of them are doing Sociology.
CHAS	So it's just you on your own.
BEA	Yeah… Still, I'm used to that.

*Bea looks at the floor. A cloud has descended. **Chas** isn't quite sure how to respond.*

CHAS	Do sociologists earn big money?
BEA	No, you're confusing them with footballers.
CHAS	Oh yeah, I'm always doing that.

*There is now the definite beginning of a spark between them. But the moment is ruptured by the return of **Andrew**.*

ANDREW	I didn't make it to the toilet.

CHAS	Oh no.
ANDREW	Just suddenly realised I wasn't going to make it, so I had to choose between chucking up in the corridor or nipping into the games cupboard and doing it with a bit of privacy. Still, managed to miss my trousers, just splashed my shoes a bit.
CHAS	Which bit of the games cupboard did you throw up in?
ANDREW	Mostly over the cricket pads.
BEA	Did you clean it up?
ANDREW	No, just did a runner. *(he sits with his head in his hands)* I feel so ashamed.
CHAS	Don't be ashamed. Be proud. You threw up in Mr Biggsy's games cupboard. Most of us can only dream of achieving something like that.
BEA	Listen, you've been ill. That's a bona fide reason not to put yourself through this. You don't have to face it today.
ANDREW	I do have to face it. Otherwise I have to face him.
BEA	Never mind him. What do you want to do?
ANDREW	I want to be in Orpington.

This complete non-sequitur stops everyone in their tracks.

BEA	What?
ANDREW	The train I catch every morning terminates at a place called Orpington. And every morning I think, wouldn't it be wonderful to just not get off the train? To sit there until Orpington... then get off... and have a look around Orpington, in my own time, then jump on another train, maybe to Brighton, throw stones into the sea... Have you ever felt like that?

36

BEA	Of course I have, everyone has. We'd all like to stay on the train. Lose ourselves. But we can't, so forget Orpington, ignore your dad…
ANDREW	*(interrupts)* Oh yeah, like that's really possible.
BEA	Of course it's possible.
ANDREW	You just don't understand what it's like, Two-Brains. You're a star. No one has you down as a mental weakling, you have it easy.
BEA	Oh, here we go, you think it's easy do you? Easy to deal with that endless, excruciating, chorus of…

Snap transition to **Mr** *and* **Mrs B**.

MR/MRS B	We are so very proud of you.
MRS B	Very proud.
MR B	You've done so brilliantly.
MRS B	Amazingly brilliantly.
MR B	Your Auntie Jean's very proud as well.
MRS B	She's coming round later.
MR B	For tea.
MRS B	With éclairs.
MR B	And to make plans.
MRS B	For the party.
MR B	Your big party.
MRS B	You will play your violin for her if she asks, won't you?
MR B	Only she loves to hear you play.

MRS B	And she was so disappointed last time.
MR B	When you… didn't want to.

*Hard cut to **Bea** who is now in full, aggressive sarcasm role.*

BEA	Oh yes, I'm really looking forward to being force-fed chocolate éclairs and being paraded like a show pony. Oh, and lucky me, they want to throw a party for me, where Mum can tell everyone how I've done 'amazingly brilliantly' and generally double up the adverbs like some poxy disc jockey. And, if I'm really lucky, they might even get up and dance!

Hard lighting and music cut as Abba's Dancing Queen *booms out and we see **Mr** and **Mrs B** doing their embarrassing parental dancing. Abba: 'You can dance/You can jive/Having the time of your life…'*

The lights and music disappear as suddenly as they began.

BEA	*(continues)* That's something to look forward to. Yes, it's just great… being suffocated and… and smothered with… with *(can't find the word)* … treacle.
ANDREW	Treacle?
BEA	*(shouts)* Yes! Toxic treacle!

*Andrew has been taken aback by the vehemence of her feelings. The silence is broken by **Chas**.*

CHAS	*(as a sports commentator)* And you join us here live for the World Heavyweight Whinging Championships.

*Andrew and Bea feel ashamed. Suddenly **Miss Baxendale** flutters in.*

MISS BAXENDALE	Sorry about that, found the key. On the wrong hook and in the wrong cupboard but heigh-ho,

such is life. I'm so sorry about the delay, sorry, and sorry about the silly scene earlier. Been a bit under the weather, sorry. *(she mimes opening the door)* Aha! Open sesame, in you go. Are you okay, Andrew? You don't look very good.

ANDREW   Um, I'm fine, miss. Thanks.

MISS BAXENDALE Okay, you three go in and get yourselves settled. I'll be in to hand out your exam papers shortly. *(she starts to move off)*

BEA   *(exasperation)* Where are you going now, miss?

MISS BAXENDALE I promised Mr Biggs I'd just give him a quick hand. Someone's had a bit of an accident in his games cupboard. *(as she leaves)* Go on, go on, go through, make yourselves at home, shan't be a tick. *(she exits)*

Hesitantly **Bea** and **Chas** move towards the exam room. **Andrew** stands frozen to the spot.

BEA   Are you coming?

Black out.

Scene Two

In the black out the actors portraying the parents are stagehands as they position three desks (with chairs) in a triangle. One chair is in the foreground, two slightly further upstage.

Another chair is placed at the front of the stage off to one side. As they move this furniture into place, the parents quietly deliver a 'round' of parental advice, each line beginning before the previous one ends, as follows:

Mr A	Always read the question.
Mrs A	And read it carefully.
Mr A	Always very carefully.
Mr B	We know you'll do well.
Mrs B	You always do so well.
Mr B	We are so proud of you.
Mrs C	Just try not to cock it up.
Mr A	Always check what you've done.
Mrs C	You're such a silly sod.
Mr A	Allow time, at the end…
Mrs A	… to check what you've done.
Mr A	Don't get panicky.
Mrs A	Treat it as a challenge.
Mr A	Don't flake.
Mrs A	An exciting challenge.
Mrs B	There'll be an éclair.
Mr B	Many éclairs.
Mrs B	Ready and waiting.
Mr B	And Auntie Jean.

MRS B	She's so proud of you.
MR B	Everyone is.
MRS C	For God's sake concentrate.
MRS B	So very proud.
MRS C	That's all I ask.
MR A	Remember, tiger…
MRS A	All the best.
MR A	… don't let yourself down.
MRS A	The very best.
MR A	Just up to you.
MRS B	We're all so proud.
MR A	This is where you find out…
MR B	You're our star.
MR A	… about yourself.

*When the lights come up there are three desks centre-stage with **Andrew** sitting at the front desk, the apex of the triangle, and **Bea** and **Chas** at the two desks behind.*

*The exam papers are face down on the desks. **Andrew** is looking horribly tense as **Miss Baxendale** walks between the desks giving them a final briefing. The chair she will sit on is off to the side.*

MISS BAXENDALE	Remember to keep an eye on the time. If anyone has a problem, just put up your hand. Very well. *(she heads towards her invigilator's chair)* You may now turn over your… Oh sorry, sorry, forgot something, sorry…

*Bea and Chas stop halfway through the act of turning over their exam papers. They look at each other in exasperation. **Andrew**, by contrast, has not moved a muscle and seems to be almost in a trance.*

Sorry. I meant to say make sure what you write is neat and legible. There's no point getting something right if no one can read it. Right, okay... sorry, just wanted to say that. And now *(she walks towards her chair)* you may turn over your papers.

She sits down, takes a paperback out of her bag and starts to read. Meanwhile, **Bea** *and* **Chas** *turn over their papers and start to read the rubric. Slowly they become aware of the fact that ahead of them,* **Andrew** *has still not moved a muscle. They share looks of concern.* **Bea** *gives* **Chas** *a look as if to say 'Do something'.* **Chas** *isn't sure what to do. Eventually he leans forward and gently lobs a rubber that hits* **Andrew** *on the shoulder, but* **Andrew** *doesn't register it at all.* **Bea** *and* **Chas** *share another look, then* **Chas** *raises his arm in the air.* **Miss Baxendale** *doesn't notice him, just keeps her nose in her book and does her nervous throat-clearing cough.*

Chas *starts to click his fingers to get her attention. She looks up.*

MISS BAXENDALE   Yes?

CHAS   Um, I've dropped my rubber, can I go and pick it up please, miss?

MISS BAXENDALE   *(a little perplexed)* Yes.

Chas *comes forward and kneels down next to* **Andrew** *under the pretext of retrieving his rubber.*

CHAS   Are you okay? *(no response)* My mouth doesn't look like a broken bottle, does it? *(still **Andrew** doesn't respond)* Andrew...

MISS BAXENDALE   No whispering.

Slowly **Chas** *heads back towards his desk. As he does so,* **Miss Baxendale** *initiates another irritating flurry of throat-clearing coughs.*

CHAS   I've got some throat sweets, miss, if you'd like one.

MISS BAXENDALE   What?

CHAS   Throat sweets... for that cough.

MISS BAXENDALE *(mystified)* What cough?

Chas and Bea share a look of exasperation.

CHAS   *(mutters)* Doesn't matter, miss.

Miss Baxendale notices the inert Andrew.

MISS BAXENDALE Andrew... *(she approaches him)* Andrew... *(he looks at her)* Is there a problem?

ANDREW   *(robotically)* No, miss.

MISS BAXENDALE Only you don't seem to have turned your paper over.

ANDREW   Don't I?

Andrew stares at the untouched exam paper for a few moments. Then suddenly turns it over. As he does so, the rest of the stage goes dark as his face is picked out exclusively in a tight, single spot. There is a feeling that we are now inside Andrew's head.

> *(reading the instructions to himself with occasional moments of hesitancy)* 'In the boxes above, write your centre number, candidate number, surname and initials, signature...'

The spot suddenly transfers to Chas, as the only lit figure on stage. He too is scanning the rubric.

CHAS   '... and the date. Show all stages in any calculation. Supplementary...'

Again, the spot switches to Bea as she reads the rubric. Her audio heartbeat is now barely audible. She is calm and collected.

BEA   '... answer sheets may be used. Work steadily through...'

*Suddenly her mouth is miming the words but the words are spoken by an elegant, smooth male voice, her imagined voice of the exam, **Ex**.*

Slowly another spotlight comes up on a chair, positioned, preferably, quite high on a rostrum upstage. The chair is a swivel chair, with the back towards us. We cannot see the occupant, just his sinister, arm stroking a stuffed white cat. His voice should be miked, so that it fills the theatre smoothly. (If the resource is available, the voice could be synchronised to the lighting.)

Ex	… the paper. Do not spend too long on one question.' So, my dear… we meet again.
Bea	*(with relish)* Let's have your first question, loser.
Ex	Very well. 'Is the family a social or biological grouping?'
Bea	Is that your best shot? You're dead meat. *(busily she starts to write her first essay, ignoring the voice of **Ex**)*
Ex	It looks like you have thwarted me again. No doubt this will be yet another starred A grade… You will become even more of a high-flier… even more of a prodigy… even more… separate.

Bea stops writing.

Bea	Separate?
Ex	Yes, separate. As in 'set apart'. Different, detached… *(with sinister, slow relish)* … i-so-lated.
Bea	*(defensive)* Why should I become isolated?
Ex	Because you are Two-Brains. An alien life form. Everyone is intimidated by you.
Bea	*(pauses for a moment, then resumes writing her essay)* You're talking nonsense.
Ex	Am I, my dear? Count your school friends. Do you have as many as last year? Or the year before?

BEA	*(it's beginning to get to her, but she keeps her head down and carries on writing)* Just shut up, okay?
EX	How often do you get included in things these days, hmm?
BEA	*(still head down)* I said shut up.
EX	The party invitations have rather dried up, haven't they?

She doesn't respond, just writes even more furiously.

I bet Anne Widdicombe gets more invites than you do.

BEA	*(still writing)* I don't have to listen to you.
EX	Why not?
BEA	Because you're imaginary. I created you and I can blot you out any time I like.
EX	Some voices are harder to blot out than others, though, aren't they?
BEA	Not really.

She screws her eyes tight as she concentrates hard on banishing him from her mind.

*The spot on **Ex** fades to darkness.*

There, gone.

She pauses apprehensively for a moment, as if half-expecting him to answer. Then she gives him a little smile and gets stuck into her essay again.

*As she turns a page, the general lighting comes up on our three exam candidates and **Miss Baxendale**, who is reading her paperback. **Bea** and **Chas** are writing busily, but **Andrew** is still just staring at his paper. **Miss Baxendale** does a short burst of her involuntary throat-clearing. She looks up and notices **Andrew**.*

MISS BAXENDALE Are you all right, Andrew?

ANDREW	I'm thinking, miss.

Suddenly a spot picks out Andrew's face amid a general blackness.

> No I'm not. What I'm doing is the opposite of thinking... thinking joins things up. *(he stares at his exam paper)* These are just individual words... forming a queue... a pointless queue... Got to do something... Perhaps if I try it her way... turn it into a game. *(he looks at his exam paper and falteringly starts to read the first question)* 'Palmerston's foreign policy of imperial...'

*As with **Bea**, the voice of **Ex** insidiously takes over as he appears upstage, as before, in his chair, with his back towards us. This time he has a glass of brandy instead of the white cat.*

EX	... 'expansionism ended in failure. Discuss'. You don't even know where to begin, do you? You haven't the foggiest... Oh yes, you've studied Palmerston, you know all about Palmerston, but it's just a swirl of dates and facts, you can't possibly bring a shape to any of it. That's far too difficult for a dim little plodder like you. It's too much for you. Any moment now, you'll snap. Like a dry twig.
ANDREW	Yeah? Well, maybe I'll surprise you.
EX	I don't think so, twig-boy.
ANDREW	Listen you, I'm... *(he starts to flounder)* I'm... I'm considerably stronger than a twig.

*Mysteriously, as **Ex** speaks, his voice turns into **Mr A**.*

EX/MR A	Then prove it. Make a start. Write something. You can't. You're going to fail again, aren't you? You've chosen the path marked weak.
ANDREW	*(suddenly jumps to his feet shouting)* Oh shut your face, you stupid git!

*During this exclamation, the lights have snapped up and **Andrew** finds himself on his feet being stared at by **Bea**, **Chas** and a shocked **Miss Baxendale**.*

MISS BAXENDALE   Are you sure you're all right, Andrew?

ANDREW   Um, sorry, miss, I... um...

MISS BAXENDALE   Who were you shouting at?

ANDREW   Well, you see it was... *(realises he can't explain it without being sectioned)* It was... me... I was shouting at myself, miss. Sorry.

MISS BAXENDALE   I can't tolerate shouting in an exam.

ANDREW   No, miss, permission to go and be sick, miss.

MISS BAXENDALE   Oh, of course, yes, go.

*__Andrew__ bolts off. **Miss Baxendale** watches him go, rather concerned. She does some throat clearing. She notices **Chas** and **Bea** watching her.*

All right, drama over, carry on.

*The spot switches to **Chas**, who goes back to his calculation of a tricky maths problem.*

CHAS   78 point 4... No that doesn't look right... Start again... 369 divided by 4... Fours into 36 go 9... Fours into 9 go... 2 carry 1...

*As **Chas** goes back over his figures a figure in a white suit appears behind him and watches over his shoulder. **Chas** keeps working.*

(without turning round) Not now, Dad, I'm in the middle of a long division.

DAD   Oh, right, sorry. *(**Dad** hovers nervously)* Maths, eh? Can't help you there. Never my strong point... and it's all that new maths now, isn't it? In my day we... *(stops his wittering)*

CHAS	Look, Dad, I don't mean to be rude… It's lovely to see you and everything, but Maths is probably the only GCSE I can pass and I really want to…
DAD	*(interrupts)* Nope, it's okay, I understand, your old dad's in the way. I'm always in the way. Just ask that bus driver. *(laughs self-consciously)*
CHAS	You're not in the way, it's just… Well, why are you here?
DAD	*(goes to say something, then dries)* Do you know it's gone completely out of my head. I know there was something…
CHAS	You've chosen a really bad moment.
DAD	Have I? Maybe the moment chose me.
CHAS	Eh?
DAD	Well, I think it's whenever you get really anxious that… somehow… I get sort of summoned.
CHAS	Oh, I see, so does that make you *(remembering Bea's words)* a projection of my subconscious mind?
DAD	Could be.
CHAS	Or are you a, y'know, a proper supernatural being from another world?
DAD	I wish I knew.
CHAS	*(annoyed)* You must have some idea!
DAD	Why? I'm not management, I've no idea what I am. Or why.
CHAS	*(going back to exam)* Look, I really need to get on.
DAD	I don't understand any of this. I mean, why am I all in white? I've never liked white. White makes me look fat. Always has done.

48

CHAS	*(still working)* Dad, please.
DAD	And I certainly wasn't wearing white when that bus hit me. Perhaps I should have been... maybe he'd have spotted me earlier.
CHAS	Look, Dad, I really want to do well in this.
DAD	I know, I know, I'm just saying none of this makes any sense to me either, that's all. I mean, how come you're the only one who can see me? Why can't this lot hear you talking to me?
CHAS	Dad, I'm trying to concentrate.
DAD	I know, I know, I'll shut up, sorry, it just gets to me sometimes.

Chas cracks on with his calculation, muttering occasional numbers, but he becomes increasingly aware of his dad's ghost, standing self-consciously behind him.

CHAS	*(without turning round)* Why haven't you gone?
DAD	I'm lending moral support.
CHAS	Dad, I don't need your support.
DAD	Well, that's not what you said when you were on that date last month, is it, eh? You appreciated my support then, didn't you?
CHAS	Dad...
DAD	When I gave you the advice about that bra strap...
CHAS	Yes, but...
DAD	You'd have been fumbling away for hours. And then there was the useful tip about telling them you love them!
CHAS	*(exasperated)* Dad! Leave me alone! I really want to do well in this!

DAD	Right, sorry. *(he motions to leave)*
CHAS	Could be important for my future.
DAD	*(stops, as he sets off)* Oh that's what it was, I remember now.
CHAS	Eh?
DAD	Your future. I just came to tell you that everything's going to be all right.
CHAS	*(thrown)* Everything's going to be all right?
DAD	*(quick and casual)* Yeah, your future's going to be really happy, just thought you might like to know, 'cos you seemed a bit worried about it, anyway, see ya!
CHAS	But wait a minute, I want…

Too late. **Dad** *has disappeared, leaving* **Chas** *frustrated.*

That is so typical… always buggering off when I need him…

We hear **Miss Baxendale's** *raised voice, which brings up the general lighting.*

MISS BAXENDALE You have one hour fifteen minutes remaining. *(couple of throat-clears)*

Bea *turns over a page and the tight spot returns to her. She continues to write with impressive speed.* **Ex's** *voice returns, but this time he is not lit (or barely lit).*

EX	*(voice only)* I'm still here.
BEA	*(continues writing)* I'm not listening. You're just the voice of self-doubt.
EX	Are you sure you're right about that?
BEA	*(still writing)* I'm not listening… and I'm not imagining you in the chair with the cat any more. In fact I'm not picturing you at all.

50

Ex	Oh dear, I can see I'm no match for you.
Bea	That's right, pal.
Ex	You're one of life's winners, aren't you? You're going to be a huge success... probably very rich... and very thin...

She stops writing for a beat as he's hit a nerve.

	You'll probably own a lovely big house... a long way away from your parents. You'd rather like that, wouldn't you? It'd save all those uncomfortable conversations.
Bea	For your information, I love my parents, actually.
Ex	You love them.
Bea	Yes.
Ex	But you're deeply embarrassed by them.
Bea	*(losing confidence)* I don't know what you're talking about.
Ex	Yes you do, they make you cringe.
Bea	You're talking out of your backside.
Ex	I'm a disembodied voice, I don't have a backside.
Bea	My parents and I are... are just fine, okay?
Ex	Then why won't you allow them to be proud of you?
Bea	*(genuinely lost for an answer)* Well I... I ...
Ex	They are so proud, poor dears, they've placed you on that very high pedestal... Trouble is, from up there, they do look awfully small to you, don't they? And getting smaller all the time. And further away. Like your friends. Everyone's drifting further away as you get higher and higher... and lonelier and...

BEA	*(briskly cutting him off)* Right, that's enough. *(covers her ears)* I'm not listening.

*Again **Miss Baxendale's** voice throws the lighting wide.*

MISS BAXENDALE	Andrew? Are you all right now?

***Andrew** is hesitating on the edge of the lit area. **Miss Baxendale** approaches him, lowers her voice.*

	You don't look right. Do you still feel sick?
ANDREW	No, I made it to the toilets.
MISS BAXENDALE	Good. That's good. Well done. *(she looks at him compassionately)* It's not worth making yourself ill over, y'know. You've got nothing to prove.
ANDREW	Yes I have.

He trudges a little weakly to his desk and sits down. The others watch him with concern.

*The ghost of **Dad** materialises behind **Chas**. The lighting homes in on them.*

DAD	There was something else.
CHAS	What?
DAD	Something else I meant to say, what was it now?
CHAS	You know you said my future is a happy one?
DAD	Eh? Oh, yeah.
CHAS	Well how can you possibly know that?
DAD	Well I can see into the future, can't I? *(chas looks dumbstruck)* Sorry, haven't I mentioned that before?
CHAS	No, I don't think you have.
DAD	Oh, right, I lose track.

CHAS	How can you see into the future?
DAD	Well I don't know, do I? I told you, I don't understand how any of this stuff works. Now, what was the other thing I wanted to say? My memory never used to be this bad, or did it?
CHAS	*(frustrated)* So what is this happy future then?
DAD	Well I can't tell you any details, can I? If I tell you that would probably influence your future and disturb the space-time continuum. That's basic *Star Trek* stuff. Besides, knowing what's going to happen takes the fun out of it. Like watching the highlights when someone's told you the score. I mean, admittedly, I did consider warning you not to dive down that orange chute-thing, but then I thought, no it'd be wrong to deprive him of the experience.
CHAS	Oh, cheers.
DAD	*(still trying to remember)* Damn, what was it now?
CHAS	At least give me some idea. Will I have a wife and kids and stuff?
DAD	*(still trying to recall)* Yeah, yeah, all of that.
CHAS	And a house?
DAD	Yeah, yeah, nice house, with a garden, and a water feature. Don't go telling anyone I gave you this info. People might think you're a nutter. Mum's the word. *(recalls)* That's it!
CHAS	That's what?
DAD	Mum! The other thing. I just wanted to say, try not to be too hard on your mother. I know she's a crap mum, but she means well. She can't help being a shambles. Which of us can, eh? I know I can't.

CHAS	Was that it?
DAD	Yup, I'll let you get on with your maths. *(he starts to leave)*
CHAS	Hang on, um, listen, could you do me a favour? You see that kid over there? *(indicates **Andrew**)*
DAD	What, the sort of zombie-looking one?
CHAS	Yeah, well, could you just go over and tell him not to worry because everything will be all right.
DAD	I'm exclusive to you, son. I can't see into his future.
CHAS	No, but he wouldn't know that. Please, he just really needs someone to tell him that everything's going to be all right.
DAD	*(uncomfortable)* Well, why do I have to do it? Hasn't he got a dead dad of his own?
CHAS	*(pointedly)* No, he's not as lucky as me.
DAD	He won't even be able to see me. You're the only one who can see me.
CHAS	Try and make him see you.
DAD	If I do manage it I'll probably scare the crap out of him. And I mean that literally.
CHAS	Just try. Please. And I'll forget about the four birthday presents you owe me... and the incident with...
DAD	*(cuts him off)* All right, all right, don't drag the drowned tortoise into it.

*Reluctantly **Dad** walks across to where **Andrew** is sitting, still transfixed. He stands behind **Andrew** and taps him on the shoulder. **Andrew** does not register at all. **Dad** gestures in a 'told you so' manner to **Chas**. **Chas** gestures for him to try again. **Dad** stands diagonally in front of **Andrew**. Again, not a flicker of a response. **Dad** launches into a little tap dance.*

*Nothing. He lifts his arms and emits a ghost-like 'Woooo'. Nothing. He sticks his face right up close to **Andrew**'s and gibbers. Still there is not a flicker. **Dad** gives up and crosses back to **Chas**, pausing briefly to try a cursory 'woo' on **Bea**. She too doesn't flicker.*

DAD   Told you. Whatever I am, you're the only one who can see me.

CHAS   Yeah, trouble is, if you are a product of my imagination, then all that stuff about my happy future is just imaginary as well, isn't it?

DAD   'Fraid so. Mind you, does it matter?

CHAS   Eh?

DAD   Well, is there any difference between something that feels real and something that is real?

CHAS   *(ponders this)* I don't know… maybe not. What do you… *(he looks around. **Dad** has gone)* Oh for…

*In the distance the bell rings for change of period and we hear the familiar tumult as kids change classes. At the same time the lights come up on the three exam candidates again. **Miss Baxendale** develops a nervous little throat-clearing cough, which she finds increasingly difficult to clear. It bothers **Chas** and **Bea**, but **Andrew** doesn't notice it. Suddenly we hear a stage whisper from **Mr Biggs** as he hovers awkwardly on the edge of the lit area.*

MR BIGGS   Um… Miss Baxendale?

She looks up from her book. He gestures that he needs to talk to her in private. She indicates that she can't leave her post. He beckons her more forcefully. Reluctantly, with some throat-clearing, she crosses to join him.

MISS BAXENDALE I'm invigilating.

MR BIGGS   I know, but, um… look, can we step outside and talk for a moment.

MISS BAXENDALE I can't, I'm invigilating.

MR BIGGS	*(suppressing his irritation)* Yes, you've said that, Emily, it's just… well this is rather urgent… extremely urgent in fact.

She casts a furtive glance over her shoulder. **Bea** *and* **Chas**, *who've been earwigging, pretend to get on with their work.* **Mr Biggs** *and* **Miss Baxendale** *exit together.* **Chas** *glances across to* **Andrew**, *who is still motionless.*

CHAS	*(to* **Bea***)* He still hasn't written anything.

Now **Chas** *notices that* **Bea** *has put down her pen and is sitting with her head in her hands.*

	Are you okay?
BEA	Sure. Just trying to come up with a rhyme.
CHAS	A rhyme?
BEA	For this limerick. 'There was a young woman from Putney, who stuffed both her nostrils with chutney…' But now I've lumbered myself with this 'utney' thing for the last line.
CHAS	*(interrupts)* You're writing limericks?
BEA	Yeah.
CHAS	Is that part of the Sociology exam then?
BEA	*(chuckles)* No.
CHAS	Don't waste time messing about. It'll affect your pass mark.
BEA	I'm not after a pass mark.
CHAS	Eh?

Bea *leans back in her chair and clasps her hands behind her head in a slightly forced show of relaxation.*

BEA	I've decided to fail for once. I'm tired of being 'Two-Brains'.

CHAS	For someone so bright, you're really stupid, do you know that?
BEA	I beg your pardon.
CHAS	You can't just deliberately fail an exam.
BEA	Why not?
CHAS	Because it's an insult.
BEA	An insult?
CHAS	Yes, it's an insult to all us thickos and plodders, who have to work like mad just to scrape an E, if someone with brains and ability deliberately fails just as some… some selfish, cheap thrill. *(he turns to **Andrew** for support)* That's right isn't it, Andy?

No response.

	Oh god, he's really off with the fairies.
BEA	*(inflating with rage)* It is not a selfish, cheap thrill.
CHAS	So, you fail in Sociology. Ooh, how daring! Like that's really going to put a dent in your prospects.
BEA	My prospects are…
CHAS	… brilliant. Doors will always open for you. You're clever. Life'll be a doddle.
BEA	*(getting upset)* That's rubbish, life's hard when you're clever.
CHAS	Oh yeah? How's that then?
BEA	Because clever people are never free. You're always… *(hunts for a word)* hedged in by expectations… always having your story written for you… always waiting to disappoint people.
CHAS	There are worse things.

BEA	Clever people are misfits. They're… they're afflicted with thinking, so they never have the knack of just… just surrendering to the moment and feeling happy. They analyse and mentally pick away at all their scabs until they end up in therapy groups spilling their guts out to total strangers.
CHAS	So what are you saying? That stupid people are lucky because they're too stupid to realise they're miserable, is that what you're saying?
BEA	No, no, I…
CHAS	Because we stupid people get stressed as well, y'know, we just can't afford the therapy.
BEA	You're not stupid. You just pretend to be. *(her tone becomes more glum)* And, anyway, you're the one whose life is going to be a doddle, because you can talk to people. That's better than being clever any day. Everyone likes you.
CHAS	Oh, right, so everyone likes me, do they?
BEA	Yes.
CHAS	And I suppose that's your roundabout way of asking me out for a date?

Bea is completely thrown by Chas's ingenious change of tack.

BEA	Well, I…
CHAS	All right, you suckered me into it. I'd have caved in sooner or later. Those beautiful eyes would have got me in the end.

Bea tucks her hair behind her ears and starts to turn very girly.

BEA	You like my eyes then?
CHAS	Of course I do. Any bloke would. They're gorgeous. How about Saturday?

BEA	Um… okay, yeah… that'll be nice.
CHAS	Yes, it will. There's just one thing though. I only go out with winners. I don't date twonkpots who think it's cool to take a dive in an exam.

*Bea breaks into a smile. She realises what **Chas** has been up to. And she likes it.*

BEA	Fair enough.

She turns round, scrunches up her limerick and starts tackling her exam proper.

	'Twonkpot'?
CHAS	No more talking, please, I've got an E to get.

*They resume work on their exam, but become aware of **Mr Biggs** and **Miss Baxendale** offstage having an increasingly animated conversation. We can't quite pick out exactly what **Mr Biggs** is saying, but **Miss Baxendale** is getting clearer, louder and angrier.*

MISS BAXENDALE	*(off)* Well it's understandable if I'm getting a tad upset, Michael.

Anxious male mumbling.

Yes, well I resent the word 'hysterical', I don't see why it's 'hysterical' to expect someone to keep their promises.

*Now we can discern **Mr Biggs**, and by now even **Andrew** is aware of the row.*

MR BIGGS	Emily, calm down.
MISS BAXENDALE	I will not calm down, what does it matter if she knows? If everyone knows? You've always said your marriage was a sham.

*Some disgruntled mumblings from **Mr Biggs**.*

> You did say that, Michael, you did, in the Holiday Inn in Slough, on one of our Tuesdays, I have a distinct memory of you saying your marriage was a sham and that you wished you could be with me all the time. Well, now that can happen, can't it?

__Mr Biggs__ mumbles what sounds like an evasive answer but the words aren't quite clear. The three kids all lean to that side to try to pick more of it up. Suddenly we hear a slap.

> You lying two-faced git! How could I be so totally stupid! I thought I meant something to you, but now I realise I was just your… I hate myself for being such an imbecile. I hope you rot in hell, Mr Michael Biggs. I've been humiliated.

CHAS See? Happens to everyone.

*All of a sudden **Miss Baxendale** stomps back into the exam room. For a few moments she paces up and down in a febrile emotional state. Then she stops, aware of being watched. With a huge effort of will, she pulls herself together.*

MISS BAXENDALE *(glances at her watch)* You have one hour ten minutes remaining.

Black out.

Scene Three

*The lights come up, but in a subdued state. The parents again become stagehands, each taking a desk and a chair and laying them out in a straightish line across the front of the stage. Each set of **parents** arrange themselves around the desk as if it was a kitchen table. They do this scene shifting in turn, starting with **Mr and Mrs A**.*

MR A	So then I said to him, I said, what is the point of having a business plan if we keep changing it all the time? It's a farce. A total fiasco.
MRS A	Well, try not to worry about it.
MR A	I have to worry about it, that's my job. Comes with the territory. And it's pretty rough territory, I can tell you. Apache country.
MRS A	I know, dear, you've said.
MR A	*(exhales with stress)* I don't know. It just never gets any easier. What time should he get back?

*Mr and **Mrs B** and **Auntie Jean** do their desk and chair shifting.*

MRS B	So what did the hospital say?
MR B	Do we want ordinary tea or Earl Grey?
JEAN	I'm not fussed, as long as it's warm and wet.
MRS B	So what did the hospital say? Only you have to hold them to what they say, otherwise they'll just keep fobbing him off and he'll never see the plastic knee, poor love.
JEAN	They said it'd be before Christmas.
MRS B	But when? You need a date. In writing.
MR B	Our little star will be home soon.
JEAN	Yes, bless her.

By the time they finish there's a plate of chocolate éclairs in evidence.

Mrs C quietly sings Ricky Martin's La Vida Loca *(or something similar) to herself and practises the occasional dance step as she shifts her desk and chair.*

When all is in position there's a few moments' silence. Then the lights come up on the stage-right table where **Mrs C**, *dressed up and ready to go out, is counting out some money and leaving it on the table. As she does this she shouts over her shoulder. She talks fast. Mentally she is already on her way out of the door.*

Mrs C	Sacha! It's a take-away for tea! I'm leaving the money on the table. Don't let Ashley have cutlery and keep him away from the electrics!

Meanwhile, **Chas** *has trudged in. He plonks his satchel on the floor, and sits down.*

	Oh, hello, love, didn't hear you come in, how did it go? *(she gets out a mirror and starts to freshen her make-up)*
Chas	They couldn't find the key to the exam room.
Mrs C	Oh no.
Chas	And then, when we finally got in, the teacher who was invigilating kept going outside and bursting into tears.
Mrs C	*(still applying make-up)* Honestly… that school… teachers are always having breakdowns. *(starts to pack her make-up away)*
Chas	She should never have confiscated Gary Spackman's camera. Gary got the hump and took his Polaroids of her snogging Mr Biggs straight round to Mrs Biggs, who took them straight to the Head, who suspended them both, pending a meeting of the governors. Least, that's the rumour.

Mrs C	*(hasn't really listened to a word)* How did you get on with your Maths?
Chas	Well, all right, I think, in the end.
Mrs C	You think you did all right?
Chas	Yeah, maybe better than all right.
Mrs C	Oh, thank God for that, I've been worrying about you all day.
Chas	*(taken aback)* You have?
Mrs C	Yeah, 'course I have. Just 'cos I'm all over the place doesn't mean I don't worry about you. *(she hugs him close and kisses him affectionately on the top of his head)* You're my baby boy. *(she sets off)* Okay, I'm off to salsa classes, don't wait up. Catch you later.

*She exits at speed. **Chas** is left with a rueful, relaxed smile on his face.*

Chas	Yeah, have a good time. *(he chuckles to himself)*

*The ghost of **Dad** appears. **Chas** looks at him, pleased to see him.*

	Hi, Dad. What can I do for you?
Dad	I just popped by to say… No it's gone.

*The lights fade on this scene and fade up on the table positioned stage left, where **Mr** and **Mrs B** are sitting, drinking tea. They have a guest, **Auntie Jean** and there is a plate of chocolate éclairs on the table. **Bea** comes home from school. She is humming quietly to herself and seems far more carefree than the girl we saw in the previous scenes.*

Bea	Hi, Mum, hi, Dad. Oh hi, Auntie Jean, how's Uncle Bob?
Jean	Oh fine, still waiting for a new knee, but, well, there's always someone worse off than yourself, isn't there?

BEA	Yup. Although statistically somewhere in the world there must be someone who is worse off than everyone else and so can't say that.

They laugh.

MRS B	She's right, y'know.
MR B	She's always right. How did it go today?
BEA	It went fine.
MR B	Well done, love.
MRS B	Do you want an éclair?
BEA	I'm trying to watch my weight.
JEAN	Oh listen to her, she's a lovely size. Perfect.
MRS B	*(proffering her the plate)* Go on, have one.
MR B	We got them in your honour.

Bea *hesitates for a moment.*

BEA	Cut me half of one.

Mrs B *starts to cut one.*

JEAN	Now then, young lady, you know what I'm going to ask, don't you?
BEA	Yes, I do.

Bea *turns and exits. As she goes, the lights fade up on the table centre stage, where* **Mr** *and* **Mrs A** *sit, waiting anxiously.*

MRS A	He's a bit late.
MR A	*(worried)* He's late sometimes, it's nothing to worry about. Besides, the trains are a nightmare at the moment. I blame Richard Branson.

MRS A	I thought you blamed Gordon Brown.
MR A	Well, yes, him as well. They're as bad as each other. *(he interrupts himself when he spots his son arriving)* Hi there, tiger, how did it go?
ANDREW	Oh, um, yeah, okay really.
MR A	It went okay?
ANDREW	Yeah.
MR A	Good man, good man.
MRS A	You're a bit late, we were worried.
MR A	I wasn't worried.
MRS	Were the trains bad?
ANDREW	No, I came home the long way round. Caught the train down to Orpington and then waited for it to turn round and come back up.

Mr and Mrs A exchange a worried look.

MR A	You went to Orpington?
ANDREW	Yeah.
MR A	Why did you go to Orpington?
ANDREW	*(shrugs)* Because it's there.

His parents are bewildered and concerned.

MRS A	You didn't have any problems today, did you, darling?
ANDREW	Well, it didn't start well. For a while I just sat there, not being able to think. But then, after about half an hour, I felt the fog in my brain just clear. I worked out what I should do and from that moment on I was okay.

Mr A	So you got through it? You lasted the exam?
Andrew	Oh yes. Right to the end.
Mr A	And you left time to check over what you'd done?
Andrew	Yes.
Mr A	And you were pleased with what you'd done?
Andrew	Yeah, pretty pleased.
Mr A	Good.
Andrew	*(fishing in his satchel)* You can look at it if you like.
Mr A	What?
Andrew	I brought it home with me.
Mrs A	You brought it home?
Andrew	Yeah.
Mr A	But, but why didn't you hand it in?
Andrew	*(producing a sheet of A4)* Well there was no point handing it in. *(he hands the sheet to his dad)* Not in a History exam.

Mr A is now standing transfixed by the sheet of paper he's holding. Mrs A watches her husband apprehensively.

Mrs A	What is it?
Mr A	It's, um… it's a detailed drawing of a Harley Davidson.

He turns the sheet round so that she and the audience can see it. It's impressive and lovingly drawn.

Andrew	*(proudly)* Not bad is it? I'm starving. Can I raid the fridge, Mum?

MRS A   Erm… yeah, sure.

*Andrew exits cheerfully. **Mrs A** approaches **Mr A**. Together they look at*
***Andrew**'s opus, both stunned.*

Well… you have to admit it is rather good.

Mr A doesn't respond, just keeps staring at the picture.

You used to like Harley Davidsons, didn't you?

*Slowly **Mr A** looks at **Mrs A**.*

*We switch stage left where **Bea** enters carrying her violin.*

MRS B   Your éclair's ready and waiting.

BEA   Okay, after this. I've got a date on Saturday, by
               the way.

MRS A   Oh good. Someone nice?

BEA   He's a maniac who hurls himself off scaffolding
               and makes up his own words.

MRS A   Oh, right.

BEA   Any requests, Auntie Jean?

JEAN   No, dear, you choose.

BEA   Okay.

JEAN   You don't mind playing for us, do you?

BEA   *(at peace with herself)* No, it's okay… I don't mind.

Jauntily, she tucks the violin under her chin and shapes to draw the bow
across the strings.

Black out.

A beat. Then we hear Abba's Dancing Queen. *The lights come up. The cast take the curtain call. After the curtain call we hear the voice of **Ex**.*

Ex   Goodbye… until we meet again.

End.

Staging the play

Andy Hamilton has written very specific stage directions around his play text. This script is divided into three scenes: one, before the exam; two, during the exam itself; three, after the exam. He continually gives strong clues and pointers about the shape of the staging and what actors should do as they move through each scene.

 ## THE SET

Very little set is needed to be able to tell the story effectively. The play is set mainly in a school, with occasional rapid flashbacks to the families' houses. You need to create an environment which ensures focus stays on the actors at all times as this is an actor-driven play.

The furniture that Andy Hamilton suggests should stay on-stage throughout the performance and be moved into place when needed.

Choose chairs that are different to those that the audience are sitting on. This will help to make the world of the play distinct from the familiar environment of the school auditorium. Make sure that the chairs you choose are plain enough to be seen as either being chairs used in a school exam hall, or chairs that could be found in all three homes of families A, B and C. However, the chair you choose for the mysterious 'Ex', the examiner, should be somewhat grander and more imposing than all the others. The writer suggests a swivel chair, placed high on a platform upstage.

The tables you choose for this play should also be plain and light-weight enough so that the actors can carry them around easily. They will be used to represent the tables in the examination room and also the kitchen tables in the three homes in Scene Three.

Don't be tempted to use different furniture for the different locations: there should be a fluid switching between location and time. The dialogue and actions of the characters make clear where each segment is taking place.

Establish a ritual for the first scene change. The actors are visible when they are setting up the chairs and desk-tables for the exam. This should be carried out in stylised motion, signalling that the important event all the characters have been waiting for is about to take place.

You may even wish to play some serious music under this sequence to give it extra importance.

COSTUMES

Before deciding on the costumes your characters should wear, it is important to do as much background work as possible on each character. The actors who are playing each character will be in a good position to be able to suggest clothes that they think they should wear. If you have a dedicated costume designer, it is their job to oversee choices made by each actor to ensure that all of the costumes work as a whole. They would need to be able to step back from individual characters and check that the overall effect reflects the humorous world of the play. They would also need to ensure that the costumes work well together – for example, two outfits may be confusing when seen next to each other if they are too similar in colour.

The eight central characters should wear costumes which make them distinct from each other. A designer may want to make subtle choices about costume to suggest links between the three families. For example, if Mr and Mrs B both had a splash of green in their costumes, Bea could wear a discreet ribbon of the same colour in her hair.

You will have fun choosing an outfit for the ghost character of Chas's dad. Ask yourself how much he is in Chas's head – does Chas actually see him? Is he dressed completely in white?

In one production of The Exam, *Chas's ghostly father wore a white boilersuit*

What the audience see of the character of Ex also requires interesting choices for costumes. Would you try to keep the age and gender of this character a mystery? How much of this actor is actually going to be seen? Will the audience just see his/her back, or even just an arm gesturing?

LIGHTING

The lighting design will mainly be a combination of 'natural' (neon or daylight) lighting states for the school and home scenes, and creative, imaginative lighting states for the montage effects when all the parents speak as chorus, the scene changes and the moments with Ex.

In his stage directions, Andy Hamilton suggests many moments when tight spotlights pick out certain characters. These can be for very brief moments, such as single lines of dialogue. These moments are very similar to close-ups in television drama, when we may see and hear a particular fragment of a character's story or they may even speak directly to camera and share a private thought with the listener.

In theatre, spotlights which are focused on one actor for specific moments are known as 'specials'. However, there may only be a certain number of lanterns available in the lighting department, thus limiting the number of specials. A lighting designer would have to prioritise, and perhaps work with the director of the play to negotiate moving some actors' positions so that specials can double up and be used for more than one moment. When you have decided on where the actors are going to be, you should go through the script with whoever is doing the lighting to decide where to rig the lights so that they can pick out the actors at the moments when they need to be highlighted. For example:

Hard cut to a tight spotlight where Mr A (Andrew's dad) is giving a pep talk.

MR A   Mental preparation is the key, son. That's a fact. It's what gives you the edge. It's probably where you went wrong last time when you...

The other consideration about your lighting design is the speed at which changes are made. On the whole, Andy Hamilton asks for 'snaps'. These are lighting changes which happen in the fastest possible time – they are immediate. They are the opposite of a fading effect.

This complements the snappy dialogue that drives the play. If you decide to use a few slow cross-fades (from one state to another), or slow fade-ups or fade-downs, they will signal to the audience that a moment has arrived when they can take stock of what has just happened before the next sequence of action. This is a fairly swiftly-paced play on the whole, though there are essential 'landing-stages' which the audience will need to take breath!

When deciding on lighting to suggest the interiors of the school and the houses, think about the quality of light which usually bathes these locations. For example, fluorescent striplighting is often used in schools as it is cost effective and provides stable bright light under which you can study easily. The way to simulate this on-stage is to use very cold pale blue gels in your lights. Gel is the coloured plastic sheeting cut into rectangles to fit the frames on the front of the lights, which changes the colour of the light projected onto the acting area. The light quality in the homes maybe warmer, and a straw-coloured gel would achieve this. By switching between cold fluorescent-coloured lighting to warm straw filtered lighting you will be able to identify swiftly the contrasting locations of home and school.

When you come to light Ex you may decide to use back-light to enhance his/her mysterious and imposing quality. If they are seated in a chair which faces upstage, it would seem natural to light them from a lantern hung further still upstage, which would give a halo effect around their body, and cast a large shadow on the downstage area where the exam candidates are seated.

Don't worry if you don't have lighting equipment which is sophisticated enough to be able to achieve any of these effects. It is possible to perform this play just as successfully with one lighting state. The essential thing is to make sure that the faces of all the main characters are well lit when they are speaking. This is particularly important in a comedy.

𝄞♫ SOUND

There are only a few sound effects required in this play. During the exam there is the distant sound of a lesson-end bell and a group of pupils moving classrooms. This could be produced live by a battery-operated doorbell with a continuous ring and some off-stage voices.

The disembodied voice of the exam is the main opportunity for sound effects in this play. You may choose to listen to different people you know to see who has a suitable voice and then record it onto tape, CD or minidisc.

The play ends with a piece of music, *Dancing Queen* by ABBA. This should have a full, fairly loud and uplifting sound – it changes the tone of this play in the final moments. You should choose the section of the song which is the punchiest and don't make it too long.

Work on and around the script

⌐⊙⌐ CHARACTERS

After reading the play at least three times, give the actors this exercise.

Secrets, truths and hidden views

Ask the actors playing Andrew, Bea and Chas each to lie down on a large sheet of paper and draw round them with a felt-tip marker. Pin the sheets on the wall and clearly label each shape.

Inside each character outline the rest of the cast should then write down what they believe to be their secret inner feelings. Outside the outlines, the actors playing their parents should write down everything they believe to be true about their children. The actors playing the parents should write down any thoughts they have about their children that they may not necessarily have told them.

Make sure that all the ideas stem directly from what everyone knows about the play, and that random facts and gap-fillers don't arise carelessly. This is why it is a good idea to do this when you have all read the play though carefully.

Finding character through imaginative writing

Each character should take a blank sheet of paper and find a quiet place in the rehearsal studio away from anyone else. Everyone should close their eyes and sit very comfortably. They may wish to lie down or curl into a snug ball.

They should listen to the following read aloud:

You must *think* in character from now until the end of this exercise. Then:

■ take yourself to the time and place where you were one month before the start of the play. Imagine in as much detail as you can the room where you are, how warm or cold it is, whether you are hungry, tired, happy or sad.

- Who have you most recently seen and had a conversation with?
- Was it a conversation that inspired or depressed you?
- Did you find out exciting or alarming news?
- Did you feel the person you had the conversation with respected you?
- Did you feel the person you had the conversation with loved you, or not?
- Did you feel a better person inside as a result of having had the conversation?
- Where did you go immediately after the conversation?
- Is that where you are now?
- Did you choose to go to this place?
- Did you find this place comforting or threatening?
- Are you nervous or bored by the prospect of next week's exam?
- Do you think you will get a good enough result?
- What do you think your family want the result to be?
- What do you think your family expect the result to be?
- What must you do in order to do well in this exam?
- What could stop you from doing well?

Now imagine you are going to speak for one minute to a member of the audience whom you have never met about your thoughts and feelings at this moment. Open your eyes and write the monologue down as your character.

When the students have finished, they can perform their monologue to the rest of the cast. This will develop the actor's own character, throw up some interesting and useful history for everyone in the cast and help to establish each character's distinctive voice.

Exploring the characters

Everyone in the cast should take it in turn to explore each character in the play in a physical way.

Begin by asking everyone to walk around in a large empty rehearsal room. They should walk as themselves, focusing inwards so they become unaware of other people and distractions in the room.

cont...

Someone should then call out each character's name, in turn, giving a few minutes between each one. Everyone should try walking as that particular character. They should think about the speed they walk. They should try walking with the particular purpose they think that character would be motivated by. They should try to identify which part of their body leads when they walk – do they lead with their chin, nose, stomach or feet? Where is their centre of gravity? Do they have a heavy walk? If so, is it heavy due to laziness or confidence? Does their walk exhibit shyness?

Finally, ask everyone in the cast to walk around the room as the character they are going to play. They should become aware of all the other characters walking around the space. Do they allow themselves to get closer to some characters than others? What is their reaction when they feel certain characters getting close to them? Do they feel comfortable or uncomfortable? How close do they allow themselves to get to other characters?

PLAYING TEACHERS

You may think that one of the most difficult things for students to do is to play the part of teachers. This can be true – and there are certainly things that should be avoided, such as: don't play the teachers as clowns, they should be taken as seriously as the other characters; don't base them on actual teachers in school as this will only result in cheap laughs; avoid over the top portrayals or caricatures. The last thing the teachers in this play ever do is actually teach, so the actors should play them as real people, with real fears and ambitions.

Drama

Improvise a scene which takes place in the staffroom in which all the actors play teachers. Could the staff discussions be about BEA and Andrew as well as Chas? Decide what subject they teach, such as Maths, Geography, Science or History. The discussion should be about an encounter they have just had at a parents' evening the night before with Chas and his mother. See if the teachers have differing views about Chas and his mother. Which teachers are supportive of Chas and his mother and which teachers show little interest?

VISUALISING THE THREE HOUSES

Gather together as many furniture catalogues, homeware catalogues, wallpaper samples, car magazines, kitchen and bathroom catalogues, carpet samples, different newspapers and magazines as you can. You could also download photos of the inside of houses and flats from estate agents' websites and print them out.

Divide the classroom wall into three large equal spaces and label them A, B and C. Choose from your assortment of photos and visual materials which you think would be found in the homes of the three families. You may wish to pin them up on the wall randomly, or to arrange them like a house, with the garden, kitchen and living room downstairs, and ideas of what their bedrooms and bathrooms are like upstairs. Perhaps you will decide that one of the families lives in a single-storey accommodation like a flat.

Compile as much photographic and other visual reference for each house as possible. This will give the whole cast a detailed picture of the three families whose lives are at the centre of the play. It will also be helpful for whoever is designing the set, costumes and lighting.

EXPLORING THE SCRIPT

Before you start rehearsing the play intensively, you should divide it into smaller, more manageable units. The Exam is already split into three scenes, but you will find it easier to break each of these scenes into smaller units and concentrate on one at a time. You will then be able to find the individual shape of each unit and won't find long stretches of dialogue are in danger of sagging halfway through.

It is important that you find the right pace to start the play so that the style of the comedy is set and the audience knows where they are.

"The opening scene needs energy and electricity; it needs to announce the world of the piece. It is a vibrant introduction to a sense of place within the kids' heads."

Andy Hamilton

∿ FINDING RHYTHM

You'll be amazed how helpful it can be to spend time working out the rhythm which lies beneath the text as it will help you to find a good pace to deliver the dialogue. Work through this exercise with the first montage of text which the parents have at the start of the play:

Finding a rhythm

Divide the class into five equally-sized groups. Each group takes the line of one character: Mr A, Mrs A, Mr B, Mrs B and Mrs C.

Each group should choose a coloured pen which relates to the character that they have chosen, for example Mrs C's group may choose a red pen, to show that she is a risk-taker.

First, go through each line of the montage carefully. Each group should decide collectively which word or syllable in the line deserves to be stressed or given emphasis. This decision should be instinctive, rather than discussed at length – found by saying the line with different words stressed until the group decides which one they like. They should then underline that word or syllable in using their coloured pen. For example, choices of emphasis might be as follows:

MR A	<u>Always</u> read the question.
MRS A	<u>Always</u>.
MR A	And read it <u>care</u>fully.
MRS A	<u>Very</u> carefully.
MR B	We <u>know</u> you'll do well.
MRS B	You <u>always</u> do well.
MRS C	Just <u>try</u> not to cock it up.
MR A	Keep an eye on the <u>time</u>.
MRS A	Don't spend <u>too</u> long...
MR & MRS A *(louder)* ... on <u>one</u> question.
MR B	You're <u>bound</u> to do well.
MRS B	You're so <u>good</u> at exams.
MR B	Mr <u>Pringle</u> said so.

Mrs B	At the <u>parents</u>' evening.
Mr B	'She's <u>brilliant</u> at exams'.
Mrs B	That's what he <u>said</u>.
Mr B	'But then she's brilliant at <u>every</u>thing'.
Mrs B	His <u>very</u> words.

Each group should discuss their choices of underlined word. They should give reasons for their choice.

Then ask someone to tap a slow even beat on a woodblock or side of a chair. As everyone is listening to this steady beat, the groups should say their chosen word on the beat.

Try this a few times until everyone feels comfortable going through the list of stressed words. Once each group feels confident that they can get their chosen word to 'land' on the beat, they can start to hear in their heads how the rest of the line can fit.

When everyone is ready, try saying the whole text with the chosen words still on the beat. Keep the beat slow. You'll find it difficult to get all the words out at first. (Begin with some limbering up exercises for your tongue and lower jaw). Eventually, however, you should find that by working together you can make complete sense of each line in the way it is said while sticking to the rhythm.

Discuss what the effect of following a rhythm achieves for an audience. When the rhythm can be clearly heard, is it easier for an audience to absorb the words that are being spoken? Think of what happens in a rap, especially where the words are trying to say something important. You may be able to remember a particular example.

Hot-seating characters: Andrew, Bea and Chas

Students often take a 'mascot' into an exam, for example a favourite soft toy or doll. Divide the class into three groups. Give one group the character of Andrew, another Bea and the third group Chas. Each group should take a couple of days to find a mascot that they think their character would have, reminding them that they must be able to explain why they arrived at their choice.

cont...

In turn, ask for a volunteer from each group should seat him/her and their group mascot in the centre of all the other actors sitting on chairs. Everyone takes turns to 'hot-seat' the character in the centre by asking him/her questions about their mascot.

Hot-seating is a familiar exercise for actors. It's a good way to stretch the actor's imagination by putting them on the spot. Note, however, that it is better to ask questions that lead the person in the hot-seat to reveal more about their character, rather than questions like 'What time is it?', which could be asked of anyone. For example:

- What is your greatest fear?
- What is your favourite type of music?
- Do you enjoy spending time with people your own age or of all ages?
- Are you generous with money?
- Do you feel confident about your appearance?
- Do you think you make friends easily?
- What clothes are do you like wearing?

Writing

The actors should choose one of the three main characters, Andrew, Bea or Chas, while you set them a question that may well come up in one of their exams, although there is no need to set a history or sociology question.

Set yourself a question that could come up in a creative writing exam. They should write with the type of handwriting and the sorts of sentences and descriptions they think that character would use.

PLAYING COMEDY

Comic timing is essential, and needs careful practice. The best way to gain lots of laughs in your performance of this play is to rehearse it thoroughly and let the dialogue lead you. Don't worry about whether the play is going to be funny or not. Trust in the work that you do and, if you play the scenes as realistically as you can, the audience will share the humour you find in them yourself. Remember, though, that if your viewers can see that you find a line or situation funny, they will not laugh. So you must make sure that all actors commit to playing even the most hilarious moments with complete seriousness. Even so, you must find a way at the beginning of the play to signal to the audience that they are *allowed* to laugh. Very confident, assured performances usually put an audience at ease and help them to relax. If the audience reaches the end of the first short scene believing that the performance is going to be good, the comedy will work for itself. Don't be unnerved if you find that the laughs come at different times from one performance to the next! Remember that gestures, or the way you sit or stand can be as funny as the lines you say. Also, where you pause in a line can create humour. Even long silences in the right place can be very effective.

FINDING DIFFERENT VOICES THROUGH PACE

You may find that characters speak at different paces. Pace is different to speed. A character with fast pace does not simply talk quickly. He/she may take shorter breaths. He/she may energise words more vividly than others. If a character has fast pace, it is usually because that character is driven by something, either good or bad forces, which gives them the motivation to speak with more urgency.

Drama

Without thinking or discussing too much, line the actors up against a wall with the character who thinks they speak with the most energetic pace at one end and the one with the slowest pace at the other. Make a note of the order and then see if it becomes true as you rehearse the play.

Body language

The three actors playing the Chas, Bea and Andrew should sit in front of a large mirror. They should imagine themselves in the scene when they are waiting for Miss Baxendale to find the key to the exam room. After two minutes, someone should ask them to make their bodies accurately reflect what is going on in their heads.

They should also become aware of the space between them. How do they feel physically towards the other two characters?

KEEP THE TEXT MOVING

When the three actors are rehearsing the dialogue in Scene One, it is a good idea for them to stop at different points and answer questions like: Where do you think the conversation is going at this point? Would you change direction if you could? Do you want to divulge the information you are currently talking about? How could you cause a distraction?

Discussion

When do you think the three exam candidates begin to trust each other, and to what extent? Work your way slowly through Scene One and see if you think it happens during their dialogue here.

 ## CREATIVE WRITING ASSIGNMENT FROM ANDY HAMILTON

Write a scene which helps you to get under the skin of one of the characters. It should be an episode that isn't included in the play so, for example, it could be the moment Andrew doesn't sit history the first time around, or a day at work for one of the parents. Your scene should last a maximum of three minutes.

Remember

You may find that improvisation throws up some really exciting work. DO NOT, however, be tempted to insert this work into your production. The text must be respected and remain unchanged. *The Exam* is written by a hugely experienced writer who knows his craft and has thought very carefully about each word, as well as the structure and pace of the play.

Themes in and around the play

✐ EXAM PRESSURE – STRATEGIES FOR OVERCOMING STRESS

Here are the dos and don'ts as recommended by Childline.* Most of them are common sense, but it is amazing what you can forget or lose sight of when you are under enormous pressure to do well in an exam.

How many of the following would apply to you or someone in your class? Read through the advice and discuss them, as honestly as you can, with the other members of your class. You'll be amazed and reassured to find that other pupils in your group have similar anxieties and concerns when it comes to exams!

DOs

- Try to work to a revision timetable – start planning well before exams begin – your teacher should be able to help you with this.
- Make your books, notes and essays user-friendly, with summary notes, headings, subheadings, highlighting and revision cards. Try using key words or spider charts. Get tips on other revision techniques from teachers and friends – do what works for you.
- Everyone revises differently – find out what routine suits you best: alone or with a friend; morning or late at night; short, sharp bursts or longer revision sessions.
- Take notes of important points when revising as an aid for future revision or if you need to clarify something with a teacher. Try explaining the answers to tricky questions to someone else, or look at past exam papers and try answering some of the questions.
- Ask for help if there are things you don't understand. If you're feeling stressed out, talk to someone.

DON'Ts

- Don't leave revision to the last minute.
- Don't avoid revising subjects you don't like or find difficult.
- Don't forget that there is a life beyond revision and exams.
- Don't cram ALL night before an exam.

* A charity devoted to helping children in distress.

Mr A clearly fears that his son will fail in life. Many of Mr A's lines are assertions: "Life is tough... It's a jungle." He himself has a very genuine fear of the world; he lives very much on the edge of an abyss and he projects his own fears onto his son. Mrs A is an enabler. She papers over the cracks in the relationship between her husband and her son. Mr A has a very dominant speech pattern or rhythm in the play; Mrs A fits in around it.

Mr and Mrs B have a great emotional distance between themselves and their daughter. They can no longer find a vocabulary with which to talk to her. Rather than caring sympathetically for her and listening properly, all they can do is shovel crude advice down her throat.

Mrs C does not intentionally neglect Chas. She is a different kind of mum. She flits from one focus to another and tries to do too many things at once. Chas feels neglected throughout the play, although this is not actually the case. Dad (Chas's father) is a caring ghost – though he is very disorganised. He throws away the most important advice he has to give Chas regarding his future and often forgets what he has come to say. You get the impression that this is what he was like when he was alive.

Note: You can download free information sheets about how children cope with losing a parent from the Childline website at: www.childline.org.uk

Roald Dahl
MATILDA
Illustrated by
Quentin Blake

READ *MATILDA* BY ROALD DAHL

Matilda has two horrible parents and a horrible brother. They have been very cruel to her and are mean to her because she is cleverer than them.

Matilda longs for her parents to be good and loving and understanding, but they are none of these things. They are perfectly horrid to her.

See if you can spot any similarities between Matilda's parents and those in *The Exam*.

Drama

Devise a scene which is set in the future after the exam, for example one week after the story has ended. All three sets of parents sit outside the Headteacher's office waiting to see him. They have each received a letter asking them to come in for an appointment to discuss the progress of their child.

One at a time they go into the office: firstly Mr and Mrs A, then Mr and Mrs B. Finally it is the turn of Mrs C. As each set of parents is interviewed, the other parents wait outside and talk about their children. See what emerges. You should find that you have three conversations: A + B, B + C and A + C. (If you have a large class, you may decide that these three conversations could be worked on separately in small groups, staying within the context described above.) Then everyone could share the work. Do any parents blame other children or their parents for influencing their own child?

Showing anger in drama

Explore how teenagers show their anger to peers, parents and teachers. Working in small groups, devise a scene in which a teenager is angry about something, for example failing an exam. Have the same actor show his feelings in three separate scenes. The first one with actors playing his friends, the second with different actors playing his parents and the third with an actor playing his teacher. How do the three groups differ in the way they listen to the central character? How does the central teenage character show anger differently depending on whose company he or she is in? Is anger always shown by huge outbursts of shouting? Can it be shown by silent tension?

ADHD ATTENTION DEFICIT HYPERACTIVITY DISORDER

A child exhibits symptoms of ADHD if they continually fidget or squirm, have to get up from their seat regularly, run or climb when they shouldn't, find quiet leisure activities difficult, are constantly on the go and talk excessively. Which of these symptoms do you think are true of Chas's character?

How difficult must it be for children with ADHD to perform well in exams?

Design a poster for your production of *The Exam*. Think carefully about images that would inspire audiences to see the play. Images on posters should ignite the imagination immediately and make a potential audience so excited and intrigued that they want to invest time and money in seeing the production.

Look at the two posters from previous productions of the play below. Discuss what you think are their strengths, and how you would do things differently. Are they striking in their use of shapes and contrasts? Do they catch the eye? What information do the images give you about the play's story and themes? Is it important to convey through the poster that the play is a comedy that deals with serious themes?

Andy Hamilton wrote this play because he wanted to write a piece that young people would enjoy performing and watching. He realised that the present generation are examined far more than previous ones. He has a personal memory of a friend who suffered a nervous breakdown during an exam, and he wanted to reassure young people that their concerns were taken seriously and that in the end 'it'll be all right'.

When you have performed the play, you might like to have a discussion with some of the audience. You could ask them what made them laugh the most, and whether any important ideas were thrown up by the situations involved. Perhaps some of the audience identified with one of the three characters. You could discuss whether it is possible for comedies to make people think seriously. You may be able to think of films, TV programmes or other plays that do this.

ACTIVITIES MAPPING

English Framework Objectives (Year 7/8/9)

Page Number	Learning Objectives (Year 7/8/9)			
	Word (W) & Sentence (S) Level	Text Level		Speaking & Listening
		Reading	Writing	
74				(7) 12 (8) 10 (9) 12
79		(7) 6, 7 (8) 10 (9) 14		(7) 10, 12 (8) 10, 12, 14 (9) 12, 14
80			(7) 6	
83		(7) 18	(7) 6 (8) 6	
86				(7) 15, 16, 17, 19 (8) 14, 15, 16 (9) 12, 14

National Theatre Workshops are available to support your work on this play.

There are two options available for you:

Visit the National Theatre on London's Southbank to attend a teachers' one-day INSET on the play facilitated by a director and the writer of the play. These INSET days are programmed regularly throughout the academic year and a limited number of places are available.

Host a one-day workshop at your school led by a National Theatre director and the author of the play. The day will be spent working with your staff and students on the text of this play.

For further information on prices, booking a workshop, and forthcoming dates of INSETs please contact Connections Enterprises on 0207 452 3728.

You can also:

Participate in the current Connections Programme and have access to the newest set of plays. See the Connections website for details.

For information on all the workshops and other projects about new writing for young people offered by Connections Enterprises for your school visit:

www.nationaltheatre.org.uk/connections/enterprises

The Willow Pattern

Judith Johnson

The Willow Pattern tells the story behind the willow-pattern plates that found their way to Europe in the 19th century.

Knoon-She is the much cherished daughter of a powerful Mandarin. He wants her to marry TA-Jin, a brainless warrior. But Knoon She has fallen in love with her father's secretary, Chang, and is determined to be with him despite knowing that her father would disapprove. When one day the Mandarin happens upon them kissing in the gardens, Chang is forced to flee the palace.

Encompassing poetry, story-telling, proverbs and a little martial arts, The Willow Pattern is accessible, funny, moving and thought-provoking. A great drama text for Year 7 up.

Mugged

Andrew Payne

C Collins

mugged
andrew payne

National
Theatre

Every morning a group of teenagers meet up on their way to school and hang out on the benches in the park. And every morning they are faced with the same dilemma: take the short cut across the park to school and risk running into the muggers, or go the long way around and risk being late.

When Soph has her phone stolen, Marky thinks he recognises one of the muggers and volunteers to retrieve it for her. But it goes horribly wrong...